Note to Librarians, Teachers, and Parents:

Blastoff! Readers are carefully developed by literacy experts and combine standards-based content with developmentally appropriate text.

Level 1 provides the most support through repetition of high-frequency words, light text, predictable sentence patterns, and strong visual support.

Level 2 offers early readers a bit more challenge through varied simple sentences, increased text load, and less repetition of high-frequency words.

Level 3 advances early-fluent readers toward fluency through increased text and concept load, less reliance on visuals, longer sentences, and more literary language.

Level 4 builds reading stamina by providing more text per page, increased use of punctuation, greater variation in sentence patterns, and increasingly challenging vocabulary.

Level 5 encourages children to move from "learning to read" to "reading to learn" by providing even more text, varied writing styles, and less familiar topics.

Whichever book is right for your reader, Blastoff! Readers are the perfect books to build confidence and encourage a love of reading that will last a lifetime!

This edition first published in 2018 by Bellwether Media, Inc.

No part of this publication may be reproduced in whole or in part without written permission of the publisher. For information regarding permission, write to Bellwether Media, Inc., Attention: Permissions Department, 5357 Penn Avenue South, Minneapolis, MN 55419.

Library of Congress Cataloging-in-Publication Data

LC record for RagaMuffins available at https://lccn.loc.gov/2016052715

Text copyright © 2018 by Bellwether Media, Inc. BLASTOFF! READERS and associated logos are trademarks and/or registered trademarks of Bellwether Media, Inc. SCHOLASTIC, CHILDREN'S PRESS, and associated logos are trademarks and/or registered trademarks of Scholastic Inc.

Editor: Nathan Sommer   Designer: Lois Stanfield

Printed in the United States of America, North Mankato, MN.

Table of Contents

What Are RagaMuffins?	4
History of RagaMuffins	8
Colorful Cats	12
Patient and Playful	18
Glossary	22
To Learn More	23
Index	24

What Are RagaMuffins?

RagaMuffins are fluffy cats with a silly name.

They have long, soft fur. Some people say it feels like rabbit fur!

These cats are known for being sweet and gentle.

They love to be held in arms and on laps.

History of RagaMuffins

United States

The first RagaMuffins were born in the United States. They came from ragdoll cats.

Some ragdoll owners **bred** their cats with long-haired cats for more colors.

RagaMuffins became an official **breed** in 1994.

Today, they are accepted in many cat shows. They are also popular pets!

Colorful Cats

RagaMuffins are large cats. They have round heads and long, furry tails. Walnut-shaped eyes peek out above their chubby cheeks.

RagaMuffin Profile

round head
walnut-shaped eyes
fluffy tail

Weight: 8 to 20 pounds (4 to 9 kilograms)
Life Span: 12 to 16 years

RagaMuffins have semi-long **coats**. Their **plush** fur may grow longer around their necks and bellies.

Their round paws sometimes grow **tufts** of fur.

RagaMuffin kittens are born with white hair. They get more color as they grow.

Adults can come in many colors or patterns. **Tabby** and **calico** are common.

Patient and Playful

RagaMuffins are **patient** and loving cats. They do not mind being carried.

They sometimes go **limp** when picked up.

These cats are also smart and playful. They can learn to walk on a leash and fetch toys.

Some RagaMuffins will even play dress-up!

Glossary

bred—purposely mated two cats to make kittens with certain qualities

breed—a type of cat

calico—a pattern that has patches of white, black, and reddish brown fur

coats—the hair or fur covering some animals

limp—soft and weak

patient—able to stay calm in difficult situations

plush—very thick and soft

tabby—a pattern that has stripes, patches, or swirls of colors

tufts—small bunches of long hair

To Learn More

AT THE LIBRARY

Conley, Kate A. *RagaMuffin Cats*. Minneapolis, Minn.: Checkerboard Library, 2016.

Felix, Rebecca. *Ragdolls*. Minneapolis, Minn.: Bellwether Media, 2016.

Sexton, Colleen. *The Life Cycle of a Cat*. Minneapolis, Minn.: Bellwether Media, 2011.

ON THE WEB

Learning more about RagaMuffins is as easy as 1, 2, 3.

1. Go to www.factsurfer.com.

2. Enter "RagaMuffins" into the search box.

3. Click the "Surf" button and you will see a list of related web sites.

With factsurfer.com, finding more information is just a click away.

Index

bellies, 14
bred, 9
breed, 10
cat shows, 11
cheeks, 12
coats, 14, 17
colors, 9, 16, 17
dress-up, 21
eyes, 12, 13
fetch, 20
fur, 5, 14, 15
heads, 12, 13
kittens, 16
laps, 7
learn, 20
leash, 20
life span, 13
limp, 19
name, 4

necks, 14
patterns, 17
paws, 15
pets, 11
play, 21
ragdoll cats, 8, 9
size, 12, 13
tails, 12, 13
toys, 20
tufts, 15
United States, 8

The images in this book are reproduced through the courtesy of: Helmi Flick Cat Photography, front cover, pp. 8, 16-17 (subject); Tetsu Yamazaki/ Animal Photography, pp. 4, 17 (lower right); Susan Sanger Photography, pp. 4-5, 6-7, 7, 10, 11, 12-13, 14, 15, 17 (upper left), 18, 18-19, 20, 20-21; Juniors/ Juniors/ SuperStock, pp. 9, 17 (lower left); Tatiana Makotra, pp. 13, 17 (upper right); svf74, pp. 16-17 (background).